CARING
FOR THE
SPIRIT
OF THE
FAMILY
CAREGIVER

FORTY DAYS OF REFLECTIONS
TO STRENGTHEN AND ENCOURAGE

Rev. Dr. Beryl Dennis

ISBN 978-1-63630-151-8 (Paperback)
ISBN 978-1-63630-152-5 (Digital)

Based on a project paper submitted to the faculty of
Wesley Theological Seminary in candidacy for the degree
of doctor of ministry:
Beryl Dennis, *Caring for the Spirit of the Family Caregiver,*
DMin diss., Wesley Theological Seminary, Washington
DC, 2018, TREN Id 110-0362.

Scripture quotations are from New Revised Standard
Version Bible, copyright © 1989 National Council of the
Churches of Christ in the United States of America. Used
by permission. All rights reserved worldwide.

Photograph by Shirley Nickell McBeath, 2008.
Used with permission.

Covenant Books, Inc.
11661 Hwy 707
Murrells Inlet, SC 29576
www.covenantbooks.com

You ran the race with love and grace.

Evangeline Baromietta Morris Dennis
November 9, 1933–October 3, 2020

Francis Alphonso Dennis, Sr.
August 24, 1926–September 20, 2008

CONTENTS

ACKNOWLEDGMENTS

Thank you to all family and friends who gave up their time to help me by stepping in for me to take care of my mother, sharing in my experience of caregiving and thereby making it possible for me to take a few hours here and there to complete my research and writing. Please know how much you have blessed me, but not only me. Because of your generosity of time, this work can now become a blessing to others. Thank you for sacrificing for me.

Every participant in the "devotional project" helped to make this end product what it is. Your voices are heard throughout this work, and other family caregivers hopefully will not feel as isolated in their experiences of caregiving. Your stories add to the significance of this message of faith, grace, hope, and joy found in the pages of the forty-day devotional. God moved in your lives, and now someone else will be encouraged because of your story. Thank you for sharing with me.

To my core team of closest friends and academic and professional advisors, you gave me your honest feedback, comments, and suggestions, for which I am very thankful. Your perspectives expanded mine, and I learned from you through the process of conversation, exploration, and discovery. Thank you for inspiring me.

To my parents, Evangeline and Francis Dennis, who first introduced me to God and throughout my life poured into me the essence of who I have become, thank you. You showed me what it looked like to care for others selflessly, not knowing that one day I would have the honor and privilege to take care of both of you. Thank you for nurturing the God-given gifts in me. Thank you for trusting me to meet your needs in your most vulnerable season of life. Thank you for believing in me.

I dedicate this work to God, for His purpose and His plan, just as I continue to dedicate my life to serve Him. It is my hope and prayer that other family caregivers will be strengthened and encouraged by knowing, while family caregiving may be a lonely and challenging journey, we are not alone. God will bless you and sustain you through it all because God cares about you and God loves you.

> *Be strong and courageous,*
> *do not be afraid and do not be discouraged*
> *for the Lord your God will be with you*
> *wherever you go.*
> (Joshua 1:9 NIV)

INTRODUCTION

Developing this devotional has been deeply personal in several ways. First, the project itself unfolded as a result of the journey of accompaniment I share with my mother as I take care of her during her illness. Second, the project added definition to the calling God has for my life for His purpose and His glory in the area of caring for those in need. Third, I learned from this project that I am not alone as a family caregiver in need of care for my spirit. And fourth, I learned that the wellbeing of my spirit affects the wellbeing of my mother's spirit, so it is extremely important that I maintain good health and wellbeing and encourage others to do the same.

The responses from so many other family caregivers are confirmation that there is a purpose and plan to be fulfilled for which the research for this devotional is foundational. The project offers a message for family caregivers, individuals who are concerned about family caregivers, faith communities, and community groups that are not faith-based.

The message for family caregivers is that you are not alone, and God has resources around you to help you. God is actively involved with your everyday experiences. Some help will come to you through people who will offer assistance or helpful information. You will need to ask for help sometimes, so be honest with yourself in assessing what you can and cannot do without help from others. Every day your spirit needs replenishment that you can receive by taking time with God. Starting with just a few minutes daily in meditation and prayer will make a difference. As you honor the person you are caring for, also honor yourself by taking good care of yourself. God will help you.

The message for those who are concerned about family caregivers is to be mindful of the stress and burden that the family caregiver may be experiencing. Think prayerfully and creatively about how you can help with tasks at hand. If you are not able to be involved with hands-on activities, consider offering words of encouragement by telephone calls, text messages, or e-mails, or share with them the prayers you have lifted on their behalf. Listen attentively and lovingly to the family caregiver when he or she tells you about their experiences. Exercise compassion and grace toward the family caregiver. Be patient and kind. Refamiliarize yourself with the fruits of the spirit in Galatians 5:22–23, and let the fruits of God's Holy Spirit operate within you in support of the family caregiver. God will help you.

The message for faith communities is to reach out to the family caregivers of those on your sick and shut-in lists, the homebound, and those in hospitals or other medical facilities. Often there will be a family member taking care of individuals who are sick and have been absent from church activities. Keep track of those who are the family caregivers in your faith community and remember them. When praying for the sick, pray for their family caregivers too. When visiting the sick or homebound, call ahead and ask if there is anything the family caregiver needs. If the absence of a member is noted and you learn they are caring for a loved one, even though the loved one is not part of your membership, remember that it will be very meaningful for the family caregiver to know you also care about their loved one. If your faith community has a care ministry, remember the family caregivers too. If there is a need to restructure ministries to include care of family caregivers, do what is needed to include them. God will help you.

The message for community groups that are not faith-based is that God cares and will work through secular organizations and agencies to provide the help and support needed by family caregivers, just as God will work through faith-based organizations to augment the services secular organizations provide to their communities. Explore the possibilities of partnerships where there is a need for faith-based assistance. Both faith-based and nonfaith-based communities can be resources for one another in identifying and caring for family caregivers. The message is to reach within your communities and find ways to work together to advance the mission of caring for family caregivers. God will help us.

In May 2020, the National Alliance for Caregiving and AARP published a report titled Caregiving in the U.S.[1] Consistent with the 2015 report, the study identifies for family caregivers and emphasizes that more support of family caregivers is needed.[2] Prior research shows that support for caregivers reduces compromised health issues such as stress, anxiety, depletion, depression, exhaustion, and burnout.[3] In a January 2018 report, the National Alliance for Caregiving brought greater attention to family caregiving as a national public health issue.[4]

My research investigated biblical models of care that help sustain family caregivers spiritually and emotionally. What I have personally found most helpful, uplifting, encouraging, and sustaining is the time together at the start of each day when my mother and I reflect on a Scripture text and pray before the activities of the day begin. Because my mother and I look to God for strength and courage to face whatever lies before us, the research question initially posed was "How will a forty-day devotional based on biblical models of care provide spiritual and emotional support to other family caregivers and the people who care about them?" As discussions took place with family caregivers, it became apparent that the more fruitful line of inquiry was "What do family caregivers need in a forty-day devotional to give them spiritual and emotional sustenance?" The assumption that a devotional will help family caregivers remains the same. Instead of qualifying "how the devotional would help," the inquiry became "what content in a devotional will help family caregivers."

---

[1] National Alliance for Caregiving (NAC) and AARP Public Policy Institute, Research Report: Caregiving in the U.S., (2020).

[2] National Alliance for Caregiving (NAC) and AARP Public Policy Institute, Executive Summary: Caregiving in the U.S., (2020), 5.

[3] Family Caregiver Alliance, Caregiving, https://www.caregiver.org/caregiving (Accessed January 15, 2018).

[4] National Alliance for Caregiving (NAC), From Insight to Advocacy: Addressing Family Caregiving as a National Public Health Issue, (2018).

Exploring "what caregivers need" opened the research to the very core of caring for the spirit of the family caregiver because real needs were identified based on real experiences. This devotional, which attempts to speak directly to those needs is the end product of the research. The model for this inquiry approach is grounded theologically in the view that God, through Jesus and the Holy Spirit, meets people at their point of need. The National Academies of Sciences, Engineering, and Medicine support this approach: "[t]he most effective interventions begin with an assessment of caregivers' risks, needs, strengths, and preferences."[5]

Praying at her bedside, I told my mother we would get through this season of her illness together with God's help. "God wants us to be strong and courageous," I told her. "You be strong, and I'll be courageous!" That's when I remembered the Scripture text from Joshua, chapter 1 verse 9:

> Be strong and courageous; do not be frightened or dismayed, for the Lord your God is with you wherever you go.

I read the scripture to my mother, and that became the theme for our journey.

Our journey together began when my mother and I took care of my father eight years earlier. Both parents were in fragile health but to varying degrees. I suggested we should all live together to facilitate my caring for them. Just two months after we moved to our new home, my father died. A week or so before he died, he thanked me for what I had done by having us live together. Briefly, he hesitated then said he was sorry I had gone to so much trouble only for him to now be close to death. Then he paused to tell me that God would not have wanted my mother to be alone. He concluded that all had worked out according to the will of God.

---

[5] The National Academies of Sciences, Engineering and Medicine, Families Caring for an Aging America, Report in Brief (September 2016).

And so the journey began with my mother and I living together. While somewhat fragile, my mother maintained a level of health that still allowed for her independence through the next eight years. Everything changed drastically the night her health took a sudden turn for the worse in June 2016. Over the next year, there were several visits to the emergency room, many diagnostic examinations, and time spent in rehabilitation to help her regain her mobility and strength. Upon my mother's discharge and return home, our living room became the ultimate multipurpose room—our bedroom, living room, dining room, our sanctuary for prayer and worship, the place where prayers are answered, and our healing space.

In prior years of taking care of my father and mother, I learned about and experienced the blessings and challenges of family caregiving. I am one of the fifty-three million[6] family caregivers in the United States. A family or informal caregiver is different than a professional or formal caregiver in that the family caregiver is a spouse, family member, friend, or neighbor who assists with activities of daily living (ADLs) and medical tasks. Professional caregivers may be certified nurse assistants or registered nurses who are employed to provide care in a patient's home or care facility, where the care facility may offer daycare, residential, or long-term care services. In addition to caring for a relative or close friend, the family caregiver may also be employed elsewhere such that following a full day of work, the family caregiver continues the day transitioning to taking caring of the loved one and providing the necessary activities of daily living.

Activities of daily living (ADLs or ADL) is a term used in healthcare to refer to daily self-care activities within an individual's place of residence, in outdoor environments, or both. Specifically, the seven industry-standard ADLs include bathing and grooming, dressing and undressing, meal preparation and feeding, functional transfers, safe restroom use and maintaining continence, ambulation, and memory care and stimulation for Alzheimer's and dementia. Additionally, ADLs may include transportation, fall prevention, pet

---

6   National Alliance for Caregiving (NAC) and AARP Public Policy Institute, Research Report: Caregiving in the U.S. (2020).

care, medication organization, and administering, light housekeeping, accompanying to doctor's appointments, laundry, bed-making and linen-changing, grocery-shopping, and more.[7]

Knowing some of the responsibilities family caregivers carry on their shoulders, it became important for me to find out what other family caregivers say they need to help sustain their spirit during their journey of caring for someone they love and then try to meet some aspects of that need. The outcome of my inquiry is this forty-day devotional developed in direct response to family caregiver interviews and their answers to survey questions.

Why a forty-day devotional? My experience of family caregiving began like a wilderness journey and continues to require my complete dependence on God for survival every day. Forty days is less literal and more symbolic. The wilderness is that place where even though I may feel alone, God is with me. The wilderness is that place where I don't know how our needs will be met, yet all we have needed, His Hand has provided. The wilderness is that place where God shields us, protects us, and guides us. Caregiving has taught me to trust God deeply and with confidence. Like the forty days of Lent, the caregiving journey has shown me the difference God makes as His purpose and plan for overcoming challenges unfold. While caring for my mother, I experienced God's power to overcome that is found in the resurrection of Jesus Christ. For me, forty days represents a journey in which we grow closer to God in strength, courage, and faith.

The devotional may be used for spiritual guidance and encouragement even though not all caregivers experience a wilderness. Most still need some assistance as they continue in the role of caregiver. The devotional is a companion for the journey that invites family caregivers to seek spiritual strength and wisdom from God and to replenish the spirit of compassion and love within. Each devotion includes references to biblical models or theological reflections, supported by Scripture texts. The insights from family caregivers found in each "Caregiver to Caregiver" section are excerpts from inter-

---

[7] Sevens Home Care, Activities of Daily Living, https://www.sevenshomecare.com/services/7-activities-of-daily-living/ (Accessed January 15, 2018).

views and survey responses reflecting their personal experiences. The prayers are inspired by Scripture texts found to be meaningful to family caregivers.

Devotion Components

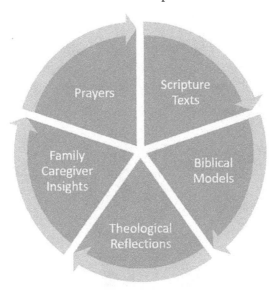

The devotions are organized into five categories—*problems* to overcome, *people* to learn from, *promises* to assure the spirit, *principles* to encourage the spirit, and *practices* to sustain the spirit. The sequence in which the categories are presented is intentional in that it represents how a training exercise for groups might be organized by first identifying the place or circumstance of need (problems), then looking at relatable biblical characters (people), followed by the review of underlying theology (promises), and lastly identifying various applications in the form of principles and practices. Each section includes eight devotions to guide meditation, reflection, and prayer. The full text of Scripture verses is provided for the convenience of the reader. The prayers are written in the form of letters to God, which allows the reader to engage in prayer naturally and easily by talking with God in a familiar and comfortable manner. Following each prayer, blank lines are available for additional prayers, reflections and notes.

PROBLEMS
TO OVERCOME
DAYS 1–8

Family caregivers find themselves fulfilling a need that is neither planned for nor expected but must be immediately incorporated into an already full schedule of responsibilities and obligations. The experience can be overwhelming, particularly when the family caregiver has no experience being a caregiver and when there are so many administrative matters that must also be taken care of when the care recipient is unable to take care of those matters themselves. For family caregivers who are also employed and must continue their employment commitments while caring for their loved one, there may be a great sense of feeling overworked. The experiences of feeling overwhelmed by the experience and all it entails and feeling overworked because each day seems to never end help explain the burden of stress, anxiety, depletion, depression, exhaustion, and burnout associated with fulfilling the role of the family caregiver.

DAY 1

Stress and Anxiety

Scripture

> Cast all your anxiety on him, because he cares for you.
> —1 Peter 5:7

Caregiver to Caregiver

I kept notebooks of questions and answers from the doctors. There were at least three. I would walk with doctors to their next destination that did not have the time to talk with me after I've waited all day or two days to see them. I cried a lot and leaned very hard on my partner at the time. I tried to disengage at home—usually unsuccessful. I also saw my primary care physician to assist with medication to help me with anxiety and extreme stress.

Reflection

When our expectations are not met for how things ought to be and when it becomes impossible to control how things really are, stress and anxiety find their way into our emotional condition. Coping with stress can be helped by managing expectations of the situation, as well as managing self-expectations of our determination to "take care of everything alone." Feelings of anxiety may be triggered by the feeling of not knowing what lies ahead and not being able to anticipate how to respond.

Prayer: Psalm 121

Dear God,

    I lift up my eyes to you because you are the source of my help and you are always watching over me. Help me with these feelings of anxiety. Help me to come down from the stress. Guide me and watch over me as I come and go. Thank you, God.

_____

_____

_____

_____

_____

_____

_____

_____

_____

_____

DAY 2

Isolation

Scripture

For as in one body we have many members, and not all the
members have the same function, so we, who are many, are one
body in Christ, and individually we are members one of another.
—Romans 12:4–5

Caregiver to Caregiver

Don't feel that you alone have the entire responsibility. Look to
others and especially to God. Make a little space for yourself each
day.

Reflection

Total detachment from all social engagements is not healthy for
the family caregiver, and God has not called any of us to fulfill our
calling as caregivers in isolation from those who would gladly help
us. Caregivers need to take courage and ask for help. We are each
part of some larger group whether that is our families, friends, or
acquaintances. Often the presence of God is experienced when we
open ourselves to receiving His blessings through the actions of those
helping us.

Prayer: Isaiah 41:10

Dear God,

Thank you for reminding me that I am not alone. Thank you for placing friends and family around me. Thank you for your presence through them. Because of you, I can reach out to others without fear. Thank you for affirming that you are with me and you are the source of my strength.

_____

_____

_____

_____

_____

_____

_____

_____

_____

_____

_____

DAY 3

Guilt

Scripture

Give as you are able, according as the Lord has blessed you.
—Deuteronomy 16:17

Caregiver to Caregiver

Don't feel guilty. Find time to care for yourself first so you have the strength and energy to care for your loved one. We don't know how much time we have, so try to make the best of each day. Laughter helps.

Reflection

It is sometimes a struggle for caregivers to take care of themselves. There may be feelings of guilt and inadequacy when exhaustion and stress take over in the life of a caregiver. Sometimes we caregivers feel guilty and stressed about taking quality time for ourselves. It can be very difficult for caregivers to detach from their loved one and trust that others will provide the appropriate care that is deserved or needed. Choose not to feel guilty and instead recognize and accept that when we are doing the best we can, that really is the best we can do.

Prayer: Psalm 118:1

Dear God,

I am relieved and thankful that I don't have to feel guilty. I give you thanks God because you are good and your love endures no matter what. I release my feelings of guilt to you and embrace your love for me and your love for my loved one. Thank you for helping me every day to do the best I can.

_____

_____

_____

_____

_____

_____

_____

_____

_____

_____

DAY 4

Anger and Resentment

Scripture

> Be angry but do not sin; do not let the sun go down on
> your anger… and be kind to one another, tenderhearted,
> forgiving one another, as God in Christ has forgiven you.
> —Ephesians 4:26 and 32

Caregiver to Caregiver

Don't beat yourself up if you get angry because so-and-so didn't do what they said they would do. You can get angry, but get over it, ask for forgiveness, and go to the person.

Reflection

God knows us so well and offers help from the Holy Spirit unless we choose otherwise. Certainly, there are times when we stumble toward seeking help from God through the Holy Spirit because our nature is sometimes more reactive than reflective. Thankfully God's grace and mercy are sufficient to bring us through the rocky roads of our experiences to where His Spirit and His peace prevail.

Prayer: Galatians 5:22–25

Dear God,

Forgive me and help me to be more forgiving. Help me not to let the day end without restored peace in my relationships. Renew my spirit, dear God. Guide me and fill me with the fruits of your Spirit. Fill me with love, joy, peace, patience, kindness, generosity, faithfulness, gentleness, and self-control. Thank you, God.

_____

_____

_____

_____

_____

_____

_____

_____

_____

_____

_____

_____

DAY 5

Helplessness and Frustration

Scripture

> You who live in the shelter of the Most High, who abide
> in the shadow of the Almighty, will say to the Lord, "My
> refuge and my fortress; my God, in whom I trust."
> —Psalm 91:1–2

Caregiver to Caregiver

It doesn't have to be a big deal, but just reach out to people that you can call and release that frustration to say that you are having a bad day today and they don't even have to say anything. You just have to. You talk to them and you cry and you do whatever you need to do to get it out so that you can re-center, come back, and be a little fresh again and again.

Reflection

Helplessness and frustration result when we need more energy for the task or when the course of events has gone "off course" and is out of our control or when the task is more complex or difficult than anticipated. It is not healthy to keep frustration bottled up inside; neither is it helpful to take out our frustration on others, so God invites us to take our feelings of frustration and helplessness to Him. God is our place of refuge, a safe place where we can take our troubles and know with absolute confidence that He will restore our peace of mind.

Prayer: Psalm 46:1

Dear God,

Thank you for being here with me. I am overwhelmed and frustrated, so I come to you for refuge and strength. I know that you will shelter and protect me even from myself. Touch my heart and touch my mind. Help me to re-center myself in you. I place my trust in you, and I find peace and solace. Thank you, God.

_____

_____

_____

_____

_____

_____

_____

_____

_____

DAY 6

Compassion Fatigue

Scripture

> So let us not grow weary in doing what is right, for we
> will reap at harvest time, if we do not give up.
> —Galatians 6:9

Caregiver to Caregiver

It's important that caregivers understand the importance of their role but also take whatever time they need to first, care for themselves and second, spend time away from their caregiving duties to refresh and reset themselves. Otherwise, they risk burnout.

Reflection

Compassion fatigue is a type of burnout where a caregiver's heightened stress level from taking care of a loved one results in burnout symptoms plus feelings of a loss of meaning and hope. When this happens, it's time to step back for a moment. Be patient with yourself. You are doing the best you can. Don't give up. Remember to breathe.

Prayer: Lamentations 3:22–23

Dear God,

Your steadfast love never ends. No matter how tired and worn out I become, I can count on new mercies from you every day. Refresh and renew my spirit when I have run myself down. Please help me not to give up. Instead, help me to stop and breathe. You are forever faithful, and I thank you and praise your holy name. Great is your faithfulness. Thank you, God.

_____

_____

_____

_____

_____

_____

_____

_____

_____

_____

_____

DAY 7

Grief

Scripture

Blessed are those who mourn, for they will be comforted.
—Matthew 5:4

Caregiver to Caregiver

I appreciate my job giving me the time to be with her every day. Just to know that I was with her every day at some point, helped me even though it was extremely stressful. I miss her dearly but am extremely relieved that she's not suffering any longer.

Reflection

Give yourself permission to grieve and mourn privately and openly. Without a place for your grief to be expressed, stress will surely compound. Remember there are others who love you and care about you. Most of all remember God is present, right there with you, to comfort you. May you be strengthened by the ultimate caregiver and our comforter.

Prayer: Psalm 23

Dear God,

    You are my guide, my protector, and my provider, and I am very thankful. In my grief and sadness, you take care of me and restore my soul. You guide me through the complexities of what happens next and give me peace. Even though this is a dark time in my life, I trust you to see me through. Thank you that I don't have to go through this alone. You are with me, and I feel the comfort of your presence. Thank you, God.

_____

_____

_____

_____

_____

_____

_____

_____

_____

_____

DAY 8

Loss

Scripture

> If I go up to the heavens, you are there; if I make my bed
> in the depths, you are there. If I rise on the wings of the
> dawn, if I settle on the far side of the sea, even there your
> hand will guide me, your right hand will hold me fast.
> —Psalm 139:8–10

Caregiver to Caregiver

Be very open-minded about what may be required of you. Stay flexible as those requirements can change without warning. Stay prayerful and trust God. Enlist a support group. Don't be too proud to ask for help.

Reflection

Whether it is the loss of our loved ones or the loss of our familiar routine, family caregivers experience loss when circumstances change. In fact, both the caregiver and the care recipient experience loss when changes happen because the experience is still one of loss. In the experience of caregiving, care recipients and family caregivers may grieve the loss of health, dreams, control, intimacy, support, security, inner peace, plans, laughter, energy, and many more. There are constant changes in the caregiving experience for both the caregiver and care recipient, and those changes can produce grief responses. While changes happen around us, God does not change, so you can trust him to help, strengthen, and comfort you through the changes and losses. God is our one constant through the experience of family caregiving.

Prayer: Romans 8:28

Dear God,

It's difficult dealing with so many changes when a loved one needs more of me than I ever imagined. Help me to make the sacrifices that are necessary and to make them with love and compassion in my heart. Where I have been inflexible, help me to adapt. Lead me and guide me as you work all these changes together for good. I love you, God, and seek to fulfill your purpose. Let there be less of me and more of you in my spirit. Thank you, God.

_____

_____

_____

_____

_____

_____

_____

PEOPLE
TO LEARN FROM
DAYS 9–16

The biblical models of caring for the spirit of the family caregiver provide guidance for caregivers as well as those who are concerned for their wellbeing. The experience of Ruth demonstrates how much God understands about the role of a family caregiver and how God provides the physical and spiritual sustenance and a place of refuge under His wings. The advice given by Paul to Timothy reiterates the truth that as family caregivers take care of their loved one like a treasure that has been entrusted to them, the Holy Spirit is right there as an integral presence in the caregiving experience. Jesus acknowledged that his disciples needed to take time away from the duty of caring to rest and restore their energy. As hard as it can be for us as family caregivers, nothing can replace rest. Jesus also modeled for us the necessity to take care of ourselves and reconnect with God through prayer as part of revitalizing and re-energizing our bodies and spirits.

DAY 9

Ruth and Naomi
Caregiver Appreciation

Scripture

> May the LORD reward you for your deeds, and may you
> have a full reward from the LORD, the God of Israel,
> under whose wings you have come for refuge!
> —Ruth 2:12

Caregiver to Caregiver

Every little thing I do for her, she tells me thanks. That shows she
appreciates me and is blessing me.

Reflection

There are so many ways to encourage a family caregiver and
appreciation is just one way. When someone noticed that Ruth had
been on her feet all day, working tirelessly, that was an acknowl-
edgement of Ruth's efforts (Ruth 2:7). Sometimes appreciation is
expressed in the form of acknowledging the effort and sacrifice necessary for family caregivers to do what they do. Whether appreciation

is expressed to you or not, God knows how much you are doing and giving of yourself.

Prayer: James 4:10

Dear God,

I humble myself before you, thanking you for your loving kindness toward me, thanking you that I can honor you and my loved one by serving him or her. I pray that my service gives glory to you. Thank you for life, love, and joy.

_____

_____

_____

_____

_____

_____

_____

_____

_____

_____

DAY 10

Paul and Timothy
Help from the Holy Spirit

Scripture

> Guard the good treasure entrusted to you, with
> the help of the Holy Spirit living in us.
> —2 Timothy 1:14

Caregiver to Caregiver

I've enjoyed the fact that God gave me this mission and this opportunity to serve my father. I don't see it as a burden. The second thing is that I believe that God trusts me to care for my father because in this journey in this life, not every child is trustworthy to do what is necessary for God's child, who is my father. There are many other people that could have been selected, but I choose to see it as He trusted me with that life because that's a life and a soul—and it's His. He says, "All souls are mine and the soul that sinneth shall die." And I believe that. It's just God-ordained.

Reflection

Thank God for the help of the Holy Spirit—not existing remotely somewhere but living within each of us, living within every family caregiver. The work of the Holy Spirit in the life of a family caregiver makes a huge positive difference. God's presence in the form of the Holy Spirit offers all the characteristics of God which are manifested within us when we submit to God's guidance, influence, and protection. Knowing the Holy Spirit is available to help family caregivers carry out their responsibilities with a spirit that reflects God's presence within requires actively seeking God and seeking the indwelling of His Spirit.

Prayer: Philippians 2:13–15

Dear God,

It is you who is at work in me, enabling me to help my loved one in a way that is pleasing to you. I acknowledge your presence and guidance. Thank you for the trust you place in me every day to guard and care for my loved one, who is my "good treasure," and thank you for taking care of both of us. All glory and honor to you, God.

_____

_____

_____

_____

_____

_____

DAY 11

Jesus and the Disciples Rest a While

Scripture

> He said to them, "Come away to a deserted place all
> by yourselves and rest a while." For many were coming
> and going, and they had no leisure even to eat.
>
> —Mark 6:31

Caregiver to Caregiver

Make sure to take time for yourself. Eat right and get as much rest as possible. Seek and accept the help of others. Prayer and faith are as important to daily wellbeing as water or breathing.

Reflection

Jesus fully understood the energy expended by the disciples in helping to meet the needs of others. Also, Jesus understands that the caregiver needs to be cared for too. Just as Jesus advised his disciples to get rest, so family caregivers must follow the same advice and get rest to replenish, restore, revive, and reinvigorate themselves. The Scripture text notes that the disciples "had no leisure even to eat."

This example of caring for the caregiver is so basic, and yet not eating and not resting can threaten one's health severely. Jesus invites all who "are weary and are carrying heavy burdens" to come to Him to find rest (Matthew 11:28).

Prayer: Matthew 11:28–30

Dear God,

I come to you because I am tired from the weight of responsibilities. I need you to help me find time in my hectic schedule to just rest. I need to rest in you where there is peace, calm, and restoration. Please help me to learn from your example of taking care of others while still making time to rest. I want to honor you by taking care of myself, so I lift this prayer to you. Humble my heart like yours and grant to me rest for my soul. Thank you, God.

_____

_____

_____

_____

_____

_____

_____

_____

_____

DAY 12

Jesus and Self-Care
Withdraw and Pray

Scripture

But now more than ever the word about Jesus spread abroad;
many crowds would gather to hear him and to be cured of their
diseases. But he would withdraw to deserted places and pray.

—Luke 5:15–16

Caregiver to Caregiver

My most common forms of respite include withdrawing and taking time for self-care, taking time to meditate and reflect and spend-
ing quality time alone with God.

Reflection

Self-care is an essential way a family caregiver honors God by
making self-care part of living out the calling to care for another.
After all, what good can come about in the mission of caring for a
family member when we are depleted? Jesus incorporated self-care
in his ministry, not by just talking about it but by living it as an
example for his disciples and as an example for us. Many caregivers

are neglectful of their health and wellbeing. Ironically, while a family caregiver will make sure the person they care for gets to every doctor's appointment and takes their medications, the caregiver fails to schedule medical appointments for themselves and forgets to take their prescriptions. Remembering how Jesus "withdrew" from what he was doing for others to take care of himself underscores the importance of self-care.

Prayer: Psalm 139:1–6

Dear God,

You have searched me and known me. You know when I sit down and when I rise up; you discern my thoughts from far away. You search out my path and my lying down and are acquainted with all my ways, including sometimes when I neglect my own care. Help me to be mindful of taking care of myself, and in so doing, I give honor to you and the one for whom I care. Thank you, God.

_____

_____

_____

_____

_____

_____

_____

_____

DAY 13

Ruth and Naomi
Total Dependence on God

Scripture

> May the LORD reward you for your deeds, and may you
> have a full reward from the LORD, the God of Israel,
> under whose wings you have come for refuge!
>   —Ruth 2:12

Caregiver to Caregiver

I deal with challenges by maintaining a strong purposeful and consistent prayer life, calling and depending on God to intervene and deliver me no matter how difficult or impossible the situation might be.

Reflection

Boaz asked God to reward Ruth because he knew how hard she worked to help and provide for Naomi. In the blessing, Boaz not only recognizes Ruth's deeds but, importantly, also recognizes that Ruth looks to God as her refuge and strength. The language "under whose wings you have come for refuge" suggests that Ruth also has God's protection because she has come under the wings of God. The language also suggests that the refuge God provides is a place of safety and even rest. Caregivers like Ruth need a place of protection, safety, and rest, and God offers all of that and more.

Prayer: Psalm 31:9–10

Dear God,

You are so good, and I am blessed that I can come to you for solace and rest. You cover me with your protection and shelter me from everything that would try to pull me down. I am very thankful and joy-filled because you watch over me. All that I need I have because of your provision. I will always look to you for safety and rest. Thank you, God.

_____

_____

_____

_____

_____

_____

_____

_____

_____

_____

DAY 14

Paul and Timothy
The Gift of God that is Within You

Scripture

> For this reason, I remind you to rekindle the gift of God
> that is within you through the laying on of my hands;
> for God did not give us a spirit of cowardice, but rather
> a spirit of power and of love and of self-discipline.
> —2 Timothy 1:6–7

Caregiver to Caregiver

Realizing that she may not be the person she used to be, meaning physically things she used to do. But at the heart, she's still my mother. And it's knowing that somebody on this planet loves you unconditionally because I'm her only child. So that love that she has for me is just still there. I know that I'm loved. I know that I love my mom back. It's taught me how to cope with difficulties, how to manage through sadness. My mother was my primary caregiver. She was a single mother. We had to develop a new way, so we're constantly growing and learning. I had to grow.

Reflection

Caregivers live out the message and the spirit of the Gospel with every act of love, compassion, kindness, and care toward the care recipient. As the message and spirit of the Gospel are lived out, the gift of God within each caregiver is rekindled, and the spirit of power, of love, and self-discipline are activated.

Prayer: Psalm 34:1–4

Dear God,

I will bless you at all times; your praise shall continually be in my mouth. I celebrate the gifts you have placed within me. Thank you for your love and compassion, thank you for your patience and grace. May all of your gifts within me become blessings to others. Thank you, God.

_____

_____

_____

_____

_____

_____

_____

DAY 15

Jesus and the Disciples Love One Another

Scripture

> I give you a new commandment, that you love one
> another. Just as I have loved you, you also should love
> one another. By this everyone will know that you are
> my disciples, if you have love for one another.
> —John 13:34–35

Caregiver to Caregiver

I pray that all families going through caring would band together and help each other out because there's nothing more beautiful than doing the right thing for a parent or parents—or for that matter, even if it's not your parents but it's a sibling. You're still family, and we're supposed to band together and be there for one another. You know that is a blessing.

Reflection

At the center of caregiving is the love for others. There is a willingness to sacrifice time, effort, and resources no matter how scarce those resources. It's a love that goes back and forth between caregiver and loved one and shared with those who become part of the care team and those who come by to visit. Love is holding a hand. Love is a smile. Love is a hug. Love is a shared memory. Love is patient. Love is kind. There's lots of love to go around. Love never ends.

Prayer: Luke 10:27

Dear God,

I love you with all my heart and with all my soul and with all my strength, and with all my mind, and I love the one for whom I care. Thank you for pouring into me your Spirit that fills me with love to be shared. Teach me how to receive love from others, especially family. Help me to understand that they may express their love in unexpected ways. Hold us together as a family and bless us so we can come together in a circle of love that starts with you. Thank you, God.

_____

_____

_____

_____

_____

_____

_____

_____

DAY 16

Jesus, the Ultimate Caregiver

Scripture

Come to me, all you that are weary and are carrying heavy burdens,
and I will give you rest. Take my yoke upon you and learn from
me; for I am gentle and humble in heart, and you will find rest
for your souls. For my yoke is easy, and my burden is light.

—Matthew 11:28–30

Caregiver to Caregiver

It was one of the most challenging times of my life. It caused a
rip in the family that can only be repaired through and with God's
help. It required everything I had within me to give. I honestly
gave all that I had, and oftentimes it felt as if I gave even more than
that, but I am so grateful for the time that I had with my mother.
In a way, it really strengthened my relationship with God and with
Jesus because what I learned was there was no one on earth I could
depend on.

Reflection

Jesus is the ultimate caregiver. There is nothing that he does
not take care of in our lives. There is no limit to the love, care, and

concern he has for caregivers and those being taken care of. He loves all of us. He understands our fatigue. He understands our burdens. He invites us to learn from him about his gentleness and humility. In Him, our souls will find rest. We can trust and depend on him to give us the rest we need. He will renew our strength.

Prayer: Isaiah 40:31

Dear God,

I am a caregiver in need of your care. I am tired and need relief. I feel weak but trust you will renew my strength. I look to you, God, to replenish my energy so I can run and not be weary, so that I can walk and not faint. I believe you are able and I know that you care. I place myself before you and hold on to you. Thank you, God.

_____

_____

_____

_____

_____

_____

_____

_____

PROMISES
TO ASSURE THE SPIRIT
DAYS 17–24

There are times in every family caregiver's experience when the situation looks daunting and what is needed is some blessed assurance that eventually, everything will be alright. The devotions in this section are intended for days when a little reminder is just what is needed to carry on. God is true to His promises, and when we are in the middle of dealing with difficulties or feeling as though we can't go any further, God has a promise to assure the spirit. The voices of family caregivers are shared in the Caregiver to Caregiver segments, serving as a testimonies of God's blessed assurance.

DAY 17

Loved by God

Scripture

Enter His gates with thanksgiving, and His courts with praise. Give thanks to Him, bless His name. For the LORD is good; His steadfast love endures forever, and His faithfulness to all generations.

—Psalm 100:4–5

Caregiver to Caregiver

God is close even when we can't feel it. Caregivers are busy, and there isn't always time to contemplate. Even when we don't take the time to go to God, God always takes time to come with us.

Reflection

You are loved by God. God loves you enough to give you the heart to care for somebody else, another life. That is an honor because that is a life that is part of your life and perhaps the very life that gave life to you. God loves you and trusts you to take care of the person you love. In the caregiving experience, we learn to trust, we learn to be thankful, peaceful, and humble. Every day won't be perfect. Just call on God. God is there for you because God loves you.

Prayer: 1 John 3:1

Dear God,

It is wonderful to know how much you love us. Thank you for the amazing love you have given us, that we should be called children of God. Because of your great love and faithfulness, we have the capacity to love those around us who are in need from generation to generation. Renew and replenish your spirit of love within me every day, I pray. Thank you, God.

_____

_____

_____

_____

_____

_____

_____

_____

_____

_____

_____

DAY 18

Supported by God

Scripture

The LORD is my light and my salvation; whom shall I fear? The LORD is the stronghold of my life; of whom shall I be afraid?
—Psalm 127:1

Caregiver to Caregiver

My mother taught us as children to take care of each other and stressed that family has to take care of family. You know nothing, and nobody is perfect, but family is there when everything else is gone. You've got family, and family has to take care of family.

Reflection

You are supported by God. Every family caregiver needs a support system. It may be family and friends, but it may be members of your faith community or social affiliation. God gives us support through his Spirit, and God also gives support through the people around us. Don't be afraid to ask for help and to reach out to other current or former family caregivers. Everyone who is on this road or has been on this road knows the journey is better with others around you.

Prayer

Dear God,

It's difficult sometimes to know who we can turn to for help. Thank you for being there constantly as a source of strength and support. Help me to overcome my apprehension about asking for help and letting others know what is going on. Lead me and guide me as I navigate through this experience. You are my light and my salvation, you are the stronghold of my life. I know there is nothing to fear because you are right here with me. Thank you for all who you bring into my life. Thank you, God.

_____

_____

_____

_____

_____

_____

_____

_____

_____

_____

DAY 19

Nurtured by God

Scripture

The Lᴏʀᴅ is my shepherd, I shall not want. He makes me lie down in green pastures; he leads me beside still waters; he restores my soul. He leads me in right paths for his name's sake.

—Psalm 23:1

Caregiver to Caregiver

Caregiving for my mother is a pleasure despite the stressful challenges it may present from day to day. This is why a strong connection, a strong relationship with God is essential to one's state of mind and to measure and nurture your spiritual barometer on a daily basis.

Reflection

You are nurtured by God. Draw strength from knowing who you are and whose you are. The Lord God is your protector and provider, your sustainer, and your source of peace. When you take time to come before God in brief moments through the day or during your prayer time, allow God to nurture and replenish you. As you pour yourself out, giving of yourself, you need to be nurtured and refilled with the Spirit of God. Remember that the Lord is your shepherd. He will take care of you and restore your soul.

Prayer

Dear God,

You bless me every day with the ability to take care of my relative with love and compassion and with enthusiasm and energy. Yet there are times when I feel tired and depleted. Guide me to times of rest when I don't know where or how to squeeze rest into my daily schedule. I know I need to be still, yet I struggle with the when, where, and how of rest. Take my hand and guide me so that I can receive spiritual nurturing and restoration from you. Thank you, God.

_____

_____

_____

_____

_____

_____

_____

_____

_____

_____

DAY 20

Comforted by God

Scripture

> Blessed are those who mourn, for they will be comforted.
> —Matthew 5:4

Caregiver to Caregiver

I still tear up when I talk about my mom, but I know I did the very best I could for her. I was comforted seeing how the people in my mother's circle of friends loved and supported her.

Reflection

You are comforted by God. In the experience of caregiving, death is that stage when everything changes just as quickly as when you became a caregiver, and you find yourself no longer in that role. Take time to grieve. Allow yourself the time and space to acknowledge all the feelings that come flooding into your body, mind, and spirit. Allow yourself moments to just sit in the presence of God and allow God to minister to you and comfort you. This is your turn to be cared for. This is your turn to be blessed by the love, compassion, and comfort of God and those God sends to take care of you.

Prayer: John 3:16

Dear God,

I am comforted knowing that death is a moment of transition when everyone who believes in you does not perish but has eternal life all because you so loved the world. Thank you that no matter the physical separation that takes place at death, the spiritual connection between the spirit of our dear loved one and our spirit remains as close as ever. Thank you for the blessing of lives well lived, and thank you for the gift of beautiful memories. Thank you, God.

_____

_____

_____

_____

_____

_____

_____

_____

_____

_____

_____

DAY 21

Blessed by God

Scripture

> Honor your father and mother—this is the first
> commandment with a promise: so that it may be well
> with you and you may live long on the earth.
> —Ephesians 6:2–3

Caregiver to Caregiver

Caregiving has been, of course, more challenging than I could ever imagine, but on the flip side, it has been rewarding beyond measure because I have lived to see for myself the relationship and connection my father has to God and his faith, hope, trust and thanks toward God. Lastly, I was able to rekindle the bond I had as a child with my father.

Reflection

You are blessed by God. Whether you are a caregiver to your parents, grandparents, aunt, uncle, or anyone who has played the role of parent in your life, you are blessed by God to have that relationship. We are called to honor our parents, and as such, we ought to give our best time, talent, and resources to their care. Even when our parents no longer know who we are, let us honor them. Perhaps their moods are varied and cause them to say hurtful words to us—still, let us honor them. Honor your parents. Bless them. God has a blessing for you too.

Prayer: Romans 12:1–2

Dear God,

Thank you for the blessing of parents and the love we share. Please help me to increase my wiliness to sacrifice on their behalf. Allow whatever time we are together to be filled with love, joy, and peace. Transform my mind so that I respond to them, not as the world might respond but in ways that are in accordance with your will. May my words and actions around my parents be good and acceptable and perfect in your sight. Thank you, God.

_____

_____

_____

_____

_____

_____

_____

_____

_____

DAY 22

Helped by God

Scripture

> With the LORD on my side I do not fear. What can mortals
> do to me? The LORD is on my side to help me.
> —Psalm 118:6–7a

Caregiver to Caregiver

We're never alone even though it seems like it at times, because God never forsakes us nor leaves us. Always be kind to yourself, find your place to release and rest, and trust God. The spirit of the caregiver needs encouragement to stay spiritually connected and to give thanks in all things.

Reflection

You are helped by God. There are certain things that happen in life that have no other explanation except that God stepped in just when you needed help. God wants us to fully understand the scope of his availability to us. God wants our faith to grow in confidence concerning his presence in our lives and the difference his presence makes. As caregivers, we sometimes don't know or will not admit that we need help, and God sends help anyway. How quickly we feel that we can handle everything by ourselves. Let us be open to receiving the help God sends our way. God knows we need it.

Prayer: Joshua 1:9

Dear God,

What a relief it is knowing that you are with us and there is no need to be fearful or dismayed. Help me to be strong and courageous as I face each day, not knowing what the day will hold. I always need your help and will gladly receive it. Help me to be all that I need to be to help my loved one. Because health conditions change, I need your help adapting to those changes. Wherever I go and whatever I am called to do, I thank you for being right here with me. Thank you, God.

_____

_____

_____

_____

_____

_____

_____

_____

_____

DAY 23

Guided by God

Scripture

If we live by the Spirit, let us also be guided by the Spirit.
—Galatians 5:25

Caregiver to Caregiver

When you feel like you have come to the end of your road, let go. Just let go and God will take control and give you unspeakable and undeniable peace and guidance.

Reflection

You are guided by God. One of the most difficult decisions to be a part of making is when your loved one needs more assistance than you are able to provide. On the part of the caregiver, there are feelings of inadequacy, regret, and guilt and even anticipatory grief brought on because a transition to a nursing facility often means your loved one will not be returning to the family home. Turn to God for guidance, strength, and comfort, particularly at times like these. Ask questions of those who can help in the decision. Convey with love and compassion why the transition is necessary, if it really is necessary. Look to God for guidance.

Prayer: Psalm 25:4–5

Dear God,

My heart aches at the thought of transferring my loved one to a care facility. Help me to know your ways and reveal to me which paths to take. Lead me and guide me in your truth and teach me, for you are the God of my salvation. For you, I wait all day long. I am depending on you. Thank you, God.

_____

_____

_____

_____

_____

_____

_____

_____

_____

_____

_____

DAY 24

Empowered by God

Scripture

> Let your work be manifest to your servants, and your
> glorious power to their children. Let the favor of the
> Lord our God be upon us and prosper for us the work
> of our hands. O prosper the work of our hands!
> —Psalm 90:16–17

Caregiver to Caregiver

I deal with the challenges by reminding myself of, and drawing strength from, how I made it through in the past relying on the support of family and friends and trusting in the favor and faithfulness of God.

Reflection

You are empowered by God. The favor and faithfulness of God are upon you. As a family caregiver, you have the anointing of God upon you because this is no small task that is on your shoulders. Trust God to use your gifts as blessings for others. In your role as caregiver, you will discover other gifts and abilities you did not know you had. God prepared you long before your caregiving assignment for such a time as this. You are empowered by God to carry out this mission of caregiving with faith, grace, hope, and joy as you give glory to God.

Prayer: Philippians 4:13

Dear God,

Because you have empowered me, I can do all things through Christ who gives me strength. Thank you for your favor upon my life and faithfulness throughout my life. Thank you for finding me worthy to serve you by caring for another. To God be the glory. Thank you, God.

_____

_____

_____

_____

_____

_____

_____

_____

_____

_____

PRINCIPLES
TO ENCOURAGE THE SPIRIT
DAYS 25–32

The devotions in this section lift up truths that will give family caregivers a firm foundation to stand on during days of uncertainty and insecurity. Principles to encourage the spirit are unwavering, faith-building devotions to remind us that with God we stand on a firm unshakable foundation and affirm what is possible in the face of unlikely circumstances. It is amazing and inspiring to hear the stories of caregivers who have weathered many storms and emerged stronger in faith and love for God.

DAY 25

Compassion

Scripture

> The LORD is good to all, and his compassion
> is over all that he has made.
>
> —Psalm 145:9

Caregiver to Caregiver

The experiences that I had with my mother have been blessings because they have helped me to change my outlook on how I look at things. It's taught me to be patient. It's taught me that there's a blessing in caring for someone because there are moments where it's just you and nobody else. I see that the trust is there because compassion has been given and the love and the time.

Reflection

Caregivers live out the message and the spirit of the Gospel with every act of love, compassion, kindness, and care toward the care recipient. Being a caregiver is an expression of love and compassion. Do the best you can for others, and do it compassionately. Remember to be open to the kindness of others because it is a blessing to give and just as it is to receive.

Prayer: John 13:34–35

Dear God,

Thank you for placing within me the spirit of your love and the spirit of compassion. When situations become hurried and intense, slow me down and let your peace come over me in place of stress and tension. Help me to breathe out all negativity and breathe in all that is positive and good. Thank you for loving me and showing me lovely ways to love others.

_____

_____

_____

_____

_____

_____

_____

_____

_____

_____

_____

_____

DAY 26

Humility

Scripture

Finally, all of you, have unity of spirit, sympathy, love for one another, a tender heart, and a humble mind.

—1 Peter 3:8

Caregiver to Caregiver

It humbles me in the fact that I am able to provide support for one that I love dearly and who once provided care for me when I was unable to do so for myself.

Reflection

What a privilege it is to care for another. A humble spirit adds to the experience of fully appreciating the vulnerability of the person being cared for. Trust is placed in the caregiver who does not take advantage but instead shares in the moments of difficulty for the person being cared for. Often a caregiver becomes the hands and legs for the person they care for. When patience and humility work together a beautiful tender experience can result.

Prayer

Dear God,

I will always ask that you help me maintain a humble spirit. Let me wear kindness as a badge that gives honor to you. Let the love in my heart run freely into the lives of those who need help and help me to do things in a way that is pleasing and gentle and considerate. Awaken the spirit of compassion in me so that I am always mindful of how it feels to be in my loved one's position. Thank you for the joy that comes with serving another with humility while honoring you. Thank you, God.

_____

_____

_____

_____

_____

_____

_____

_____

_____

_____

DAY 27

Understanding

Scripture

> For the LORD gives wisdom; from his mouth
> come knowledge and understanding
> —Proverbs 2:6

Caregiver to Caregiver

Because of the experience with my grandma, I definitely learned a lot more patience and trying to be more understanding because there were definitely times that I would get frustrated or angry, and I regret any time that I said something to her. That was mean of me to hurt her feelings. That shouldn't have happened, and I wish I could take those times back. So going forward, I try to be more cognizant of what I say or what I do.

Reflection

We are in a constant state of learning and growing in wisdom. When we become family caregivers, there is nothing to really prepare a person, but if we seek knowledge and understanding, we will grow into the caregiver God intends us to be. In this experience, we learn to become more patient, more empathetic, more understanding of the person we are caring for, and over time, we understand better how to manage their care. Remain open to gathering and learning new information. God has plans for which you are being equipped.

Prayer

Dear God,

Through caring for my loved ones, I have learned a great deal of responsibility, understanding, patience, and empathy for others. Continue to instruct me in your ways, according to your will. Help me keep an open mind and flexible spirit so I don't miss what I should be paying attention to. God, you know me, and you know I need to keep learning and growing in understanding and knowledge. Forgive me, God. Thank you, God.

_____

_____

_____

_____

_____

_____

_____

_____

_____

DAY 28

Joy

Scripture

Weeping may linger for the night, but joy comes with the morning.
—Psalm 30:5b

Caregiver to Caregiver

If you are not prepared for this journey, this path can deplete you spiritually, mentally, financially, and emotionally. Once you have gone through the acceptance process and start focusing on the needs of your loved ones and what is realistic, the journey and path will provide you with a great deal of peace and joy.

Reflection

Every day is not the same. Some days are harder than others. Thankfully, God blessed us with the ability to reflect on memories— memories of what God has brought us through, memories of joy and peace in the aftermath of challenges. Even when the memory has faded the sound of music reawakens the memory, the fragrance of a favorite meal brings back happy memories. The feeling of a hand being held is a tender memory. All are blessings reminding us that weeping may linger for the night, but joy does come in the morning.

Prayer: Psalm 126:2–3

Dear God,

    As I reflect on the blessing of caring for and loving my dear loved one, I am reminded of the smile on his/her face, and like a ray of sunlight filling a room, joy fills my heart. Thank you for the memories of laughter and joy. You, God, have done great things for our loved ones. Thank you, God. You have done great things for all of us, and we rejoice. Thank you, God.

_____

_____

_____

_____

_____

_____

_____

_____

_____

_____

_____

_____

DAY 29

Patience

Scripture

Do not lag in zeal, be ardent in spirit, serve the Lord. Rejoice
in hope, be patient in suffering, persevere in prayer. Contribute
to the needs of the saints; extend hospitality to strangers.
—Romans 12:11–13

Caregiver to Caregiver

God helped me because I don't think under normal circumstances
that I could have sustained because by nature I'm not as patient. I
am patient, but I'm not as patient. You understand what I mean. But
God gave me the strength to be patient, the strength to sustain, the
strength to do and to care.

Reflection

Patience is a virtue that can be difficult to exercise sometimes.
But patience is integral to caregiving. There are many changes. Just
about every aspect of care begins taking longer. There is no rush-
ing. The goal is to get things done slowly, carefully, properly. For
many family caregivers, patience grows with time as we become more
attuned to the needs of the person we are caring for. Love is patient

and love is kind. God will answer our prayers for patience because God is love.

Prayer: Hebrews 13:8

Dear God,

A huge change in my life has happened, and I am holding on to you for strength. In the midst of all these changes, I am thankful that you are the same yesterday, today, and forever. Strengthen my heart with grace and patience and love. Help me to slow down and breathe in your Spirit. Fill me with your presence. Fill me with your love. Thank you, God.

_____

_____

_____

_____

_____

_____

_____

_____

_____

DAY 30

Strength

Scripture

> Do not fear, for I am with you, do not be afraid, for I
> am your God; I will strengthen you, I will help you, I
> will uphold you with my victorious right hand.
> —Isaiah 41:10

Caregiver to Caregiver

Things being tense with God, I had to do a lot of praying, a lot of us asking for strength. Asking for strength was what I needed. That was pretty much my goal. And embracing that strength because my faith had to be strong in order for me to hear God tell me: "I'm here, I'm here. I'm giving you the strength. You're going to get through this. It's going to be okay." I don't think that I would have been able to if my faith was not there.

Reflection

Caregiving increases our awareness of the human condition in which we experience the love of God for each and every one of us despite our frailties, weaknesses, and conditions. Know that to need someone or depend on others is not a weakness. God builds us up in spiritual strength, and God provides others around us to be a source of strength for us. Trust God for the strength you need. He will help you and uphold you.

Prayer: Psalm 28:6–7

Dear God,

You are the source of my strength and protection. I place my complete trust in you, and I am relieved knowing I can lean upon you when I feel weak and tired and overwhelmed. Thank you for being my refuge and my strength. Thank you for hearing my prayers for strength and help. Thank you for giving me the confidence I need by depending upon you. Thank you, God.

_____

_____

_____

_____

_____

_____

_____

_____

_____

_____

DAY 31

Trust

Scripture

> Trust in the LORD with all your heart, and do not rely
> on your own insight. In all your ways acknowledge
> him, and he will make straight your paths.
> —Proverbs 3:5–6

Caregiver to Caregiver

I do all that I can do with the resources I have available and then trust God to handle the things that are out of my control. At every stage of caregiving, be certain to trust in the Lord who has promised never to leave you nor forsake you.

Reflection

Caregiving is a journey on which God invites us to trust him for everything we need along the way. God equips us for the tasks even before we realize it. That's why when we pray about a situation, God has already started working it out and establishing within you what you will need to weather the storms and manage the care of your loved one. All we need to do is call on God and trust that he will provide. We are invited to trust God with all our hearts, and that means totally and completely. God will not disappoint. He is always there for us to guide, direct, and protect us. Trust God.

Prayer: Deuteronomy 31:6

Dear God,

Thank you for constantly being by my side in this journey of caregiving. Because you are there, I feel strong and courageous. I trust you to watch over my loved one and watch over me. I trust you to help us adapt to the changes before us. I trust you to give me the right words to say when comfort is needed. I trust you to provide, sustain, and encourage us. Thank you, God.

_____

_____

_____

_____

_____

_____

_____

_____

_____

DAY 32

Forgiveness

Scripture

> Bear with one another and, if anyone has a complaint against
> another, forgive each other; just as the Lord has forgiven you,
> so you also must forgive. Above all, clothe yourselves with
> love, which binds everything together in perfect harmony.
> And let the peace of Christ rule in your hearts, to which
> indeed you were called in the one body. And be thankful.
> —Colossians 3:13–15

Caregiver to Caregiver

People need to know we all make mistakes, and God and our loved ones forgive us.

Reflection

Seeking to be grace-filled helps us to see we need to become more forgiving of ourselves and others. We know God has forgiven us, but we are generally slow to receive God's forgiveness or forgive ourselves. As caregivers, we are constantly striving to press beyond our capacities and time itself, but we need to forgive ourselves when we miss the mark and be forgiving of others for their shortcomings.

Prayer: Colossians 3:13–15

Dear God,

Thank you for the gift and the power of forgiveness. Help me to let go of the frustration, pain, and hurt. Help me to see others as you see them so I can let go of the negativity that is weighing me down. Release me and help me forgive myself for my own mistakes. Let peace rule in our hearts and bind us with your love. Thank you, God.

PRACTICES
TO SUSTAIN THE SPIRIT
DAYS 33–40

Sometimes it may be difficult to see the blessing in caregiving, but when we hear such words about the great treasure inherent in the very act of caring for another, we may feel inspired to know "where your treasure is, there your heart will be also." (Matthew 6:21). As caregivers, we are blessed (and burdened) with a closeness and tenderness that develops through the experience. There is a precious trust that is forged between the caregiver and the care recipient. The strength and vulnerability of both individuals find a balance that is delicate and also blessed by the grace of compassion.

DAY 33

Nurturing Self and Spirit

Scripture

> For the eyes of the Lord are on the righteous,
> and his ears are open to their prayer.
>
> —1 Peter 3:12a

Caregiver to Caregiver

I think the biggest thing for me was not being prepared for the role reversal because she was the matriarch of the family, and I'm not a mother. So for me stepping into a role to care for someone was quite challenging because I really didn't have that skillset, and I think that I did do a lot for my mom's brothers who were adopted because they had a lot of mental health issues, so I was constantly doing paperwork to get them some kind of assistance or trying to get them situated and living arrangements in Florida. But it was different with her because my relationship with her was different. So trying to be more nurturing and understanding I think was a huge thing for me that I didn't really have before.

Reflection

An important aspect of allowing God to care for us as caregivers is to develop strong communications with God through prayer. Nurturing one's self happens when we take time for ourselves using that time for rest, reflection, and giving ourselves permission to be on the receiving side of care. Nurturing one's spirit happens when we take time with God in prayer, speaking, and listening to God. God wants to bless us with strength and courage for this journey, so it is very important to take time to receive and acknowledge the blessings.

Prayer: Psalm 27:14

Dear God,

You are the source for the sustenance and replenishment of every fiber of my being. Refresh my spirit with your Spirit each day so that I can have the strength and courage to complete the tasks before me. Bless the person in my care and replenish and nurture them also. Thank you for hearing my prayer. Thank you, God.

_____

_____

_____

_____

_____

_____

_____

DAY 34

Finding Grace

Scripture

But he said to me, "My grace is sufficient for you, for power is made perfect in weakness." So, I will boast all the more gladly of my weaknesses, so that the power of Christ may dwell in me.
—2 Corinthians 12:9

Caregiver to Caregiver

Caregiving affected me so much that now I'm not fearful of death. I watched my dad gracefully accept what was in the plans for him—his impending death—and yet every day he could exhibit positivity in his pain and distress. I saw my father, and I said to myself, "I want to be like that." Yes, it's pretty amazing.

Reflection

Caregivers need to prepare to give and receive the grace of God, the unmerited favor of God. Both giving and receiving God's grace help ease some of the stresses of caregiving and lift the spirit of caregivers. God's grace is sufficient for every caregiver as God's power is made more perfect in our weakness. Perhaps it is when we honestly receive the grace of God in our own lives, it becomes easier to extend grace to others. While caregiving is difficult, when we acknowledge that God is constantly extending grace to us, a transformation can occur where we find ourselves extending more and more grace to others.

Prayer: Romans 12:2

Dear God,

Thank you for your favor upon me. Thank you for your grace. Help me to extend grace to others just as you extend your grace to me. Transform my mind and spirit so I reflect your presence within me and not the influences of this world. Guide me to a new understanding of your will for me and for the loved one I am caring for. Together we will honor you and give glory to you. We are blessed and thankful for your loving-kindness. Thank you, God.

_____

_____

_____

_____

_____

_____

_____

_____

DAY 35

Finding Sabbath

Scripture

And on the seventh day God finished the work that he had done, and he rested on the seventh day from all the work that he had done. So God blessed the seventh day and hallowed it, because on it God rested from all the work that he had done in creation.

—Genesis 2:2–3

Caregiver to Caregiver

As a caregiver, I find spiritual encouragement by seeking godly counsel, praying, going to worship services, and through listening to praise and worship music.

Reflection

Rest is a scarce commodity in the experience of many family caregivers. Our model for taking time to rest is God. On the seventh day of creation, God rested and "blessed the seventh day and hallowed it." There is a sacred nature to rest because resting honors God and allows for recuperation, revitalization, replenishment, and restoration of the body, mind, and spirit. When God delivered the Ten Commandments to Moses, again it is emphasized that we are to take a day of Sabbath as a holy day, different from all the other days. If the spirit of the family caregiver is to be cared for, Sabbath is essential.

Prayer: Exodus 20:8–11

Dear God,

Thank you for your example of weekly Sabbath and instruction to keep it. I struggle to find Sabbath but trust you will help me to stop, wait, and listen for your voice. I love that I can call upon you anywhere and anytime. I thank you that there is not a moment when you are not attending to me, watching over me, and protecting me. Thank you, God.

_____

_____

_____

_____

_____

_____

_____

_____

_____

_____

DAY 36

Finding Peace

Scripture

> Those of steadfast mind you keep in peace—
> in peace because they trust in you.
>
> —Isaiah 26:3

Caregiver to Caregiver

The scripture I have found uplifting is Ephesians 4, chapter 1. And to paraphrase, it's just basically that as a prisoner of the Lord, I am beholden to love to reach out in unity and in peace. I think of the word *prisoner* meaning that you've been captured. So the Lord has captured me because of that, and I have the duty to be peaceful and to be kind. So that's my personal scripture because then it allows you to see that in being captured by God, you have protection and peace that comes with being captured by him which is also life-sustaining.

Reflection

During the journey of family caregiving, there are many responsibilities, circumstances, and people that can disturb the emotional and spiritual equilibrium of the caregiver. The disturbance or disruption of peace in mind, body, and spirit is another source of exhaustion, stress, and burnout. Sometimes loss of peace feels like a rug suddenly pulled from under your feet, leaving the caregiver stunned and shocked and unable to respond with grace or respond at all. Peace will be protected when we meditate on God's Word and affirm the promises God makes to every person.

Prayer: Matthew 5:9; Romans 12:18

Dear God,

Let peace prevail in and around all that I do. My spirit is unsettled sometimes, and what I need is your peace that passes all understanding. Help me to be a peacemaker seeking understanding and bridging misunderstandings. Guide me according to your ways so that we may all live peaceably as family and friends. Thank you, God.

_____

_____

_____

_____

_____

_____

_____

_____

_____

DAY 37

Finding Community

Scripture

> Bear one another's burdens, and in this way
> you will fulfill the law of Christ.
> —Galatians 6:2

Caregiver to Caregiver

I think that any time you communicate with somebody who has these experiences, sometimes you'll hear things about resources in your community or emotional support. Sometimes you'll find somebody just listening and saying, "Oh yeah, I've been through that," and then you don't feel the regret or the guilt that you're going through. And I just think it's really important to have a community, to have a place to find resources and talk to people who understand you.

Reflection

God calls us to live in community, in fellowship with others, bearing on another's burdens. Yet many caregivers find it very difficult to ask for help, especially outside the immediate network of family. Some families develop a team structure and help care for a parent or other relative, while in other families, there is a distancing from the family caregiver and a reluctance to participate in caregiving. This is where finding a community of willing, able, supportive individuals becomes another lifeline for the family caregiver.

Prayer: Hebrews 10:24–25

Dear God,

Thank you for surrounding me with family and friends. Thank you for strangers who have become friends. Bless each one of them as they reach in and offer to help me care for my loved one. Their love and good deeds are a huge blessing. May we continue to encourage one another and continue to remember each other in prayer. Let our unity and support of one another be a testament to your working within and around us. Thank you, God.

_____

_____

_____

_____

_____

_____

_____

_____

_____

DAY 38

Finding Time

Scripture

To everything there is a season, and a time to every purpose under
the heaven: A time to be born, and a time to die; a time to plant,
and a time to pluck up that which is planted; A time to kill, and a
time to heal; a time to break down, and a time to build up; A time
to weep, and a time to laugh; a time to mourn, and a time to dance.
—Ecclesiastes 3:1–4

Caregiver to Caregiver

Finding the time to be around my friends and finding time for
myself for social encounters has been a real challenge.

Reflection

Adapting to a new schedule to accommodate taking care of
another person can be a challenge indeed. Social engagements may
need to be adjusted. Taking a break may be a scarce opportunity.
Yet God wants us to balance our lives and take care of ourselves as
caregivers. The answer for finding time involves asking for help from
people you trust and who the person you are caring for also trusts.
God knows how much this is needed, and it may take time to coordi-

nate the arrangements. Trust God that he has a plan even for finding time when there does not seem to be any. Follow God's guidance. He will answer your prayer for time.

Prayer: Psalm 133

Dear God,

How very good and pleasant it is when kindred live together in unity! I am blessed to have friends who care about me. Thankfully we can communicate virtually, but I really need personal interaction from time to time. Show me how to find the time for them and even time for myself. I know there is a season for everything and trust you will help me. Thank you, God.

_____

_____

_____

_____

_____

_____

_____

_____

_____

_____

DAY 39

Finding Solitude

Scripture

Be still and know that I am God!

—Psalm 46:10

Caregiver to Caregiver

There were times I would just go, and we would just sit and be quiet. Maybe she'd hold my hand, I would hold her, or I would lay on her hospital bed. We didn't have to say anything.

Reflection

How precious are those times when we can just sit in the presence of God? With the busyness of caregiving, finding time for solitude is not easy, but if we don't mind sharing our solitude, it's available more often than we realize. Just sitting and being still together with our loved one allows each of us to enter a space of solitude. We can really be alone with God throughout our experience of caregiving. We need solace and calm to refresh our spirits. Be still and know that God is with you.

Prayer: Psalm 62:5

Dear God,

For you alone my soul waits in silence, for my hope is from you. Thank you for this very precious time to allow my soul a moment to feel restored and revitalized. As I sit with my loved one, I realize that you have gifted us with this time to come before you together and separately. Thank you for covering us with your love. Thank you for filling us with your peace. Thank you, God.

_____

_____

_____

_____

_____

_____

_____

_____

_____

_____

_____

DAY 40

Finding Health

Scripture

> Pleasant words are like a honeycomb, sweetness
> to the soul and health to the body.
> —Proverbs 16:24

Caregiver to Caregiver

It has had an effect on my health. It has caused me to draw closer to God and to see life in a different way.

Reflection

The mental, physical, emotional, and spiritual health of the family caregiver has some bearing on the health and wellbeing of the person being cared for. The journey of caregiving is not about us, the caregivers. Our mission is for a greater purpose because the outcome of another person's health will be impacted if our health is compromised. It is therefore very important for family caregivers to find time to monitor their own health and engage in activities to enhance wellbeing. Let us make the commitment to taking care of ourselves in every way.

Prayer: Isaiah 38:16

Dear God,

In good health, people live, and the life of my spirit requires good health. Restore me to health and make me live so that your mission of care for my loved one is fulfilled. Help me prioritize myself so I can continue giving the very best that I have to give with a healthy body, mind, and spirit. Thank you, God.

_____

_____

_____

_____

_____

_____

_____

_____

_____

_____

_____

SCRIPTURE REFERENCES

SCRIPTURE TEXTS

Old Testament

> And on the seventh day God finished the work that he had done, and he rested on the seventh day from all the work that he had done. So God blessed the seventh day and hallowed it, because on it God rested from all the work that he had done in creation. (Genesis 2:2–3)

> Remember the sabbath day, and keep it holy. Six days you shall labor and do all your work. But the seventh day is a sabbath to the LORD your God; you shall not do any work—you, your son or your daughter, your male or female slave, your livestock, or the alien resident in your towns. For in six days the LORD made heaven and earth, the sea, and all that is in them, but rested the seventh day; therefore the LORD blessed the sabbath day and consecrated it. (Exodus 20:8–11)

> All shall give as they are able, according to the blessing of the LORD your God that he has given you. (Deuteronomy 16:17)

Be strong and bold; have no fear or dread of them, because it is the LORD your God who goes with you; he will not fail you or forsake you. (Deuteronomy 31:6)

I hereby command you: Be strong and courageous; do not be frightened or dismayed, for the LORD your God is with you wherever you go. (Joshua 1:9)

She said, 'Please, let me glean and gather among the sheaves behind the reapers.' So she came, and she has been on her feet from early this morning until now, without resting even for a moment. (Ruth 2:7)

May the LORD reward you for your deeds, and may you have a full reward from the LORD, the God of Israel, under whose wings you have come for refuge! (Ruth 2:12)

The LORD is my shepherd, I shall not want. He makes me lie down in green pastures; he leads me beside still waters; he restores my soul. He leads me in right paths for his name's sake.
Even though I walk through the darkest valley, I fear no evil; for you are with me your rod and your staff—they comfort me.
You prepare a table before me in the presence of my enemies; you anoint my head with oil; my cup overflows. Surely goodness and mercy shall follow me all the days of my life, and I shall dwell in the house of the LORD my whole life long. (Psalm 23:1–6)

Make me to know your ways, O Lord; teach me your paths. Lead me in your truth, and teach me, for you are the God of my salvation; for you I wait all day long. (Psalm 25:4–5)

Wait for the Lord; be strong, and let your heart take courage; wait for the Lord! (Psalm 27:14)

Blessed be the Lord, for he has heard the sound of my pleadings. The Lord is my strength and my shield; in him my heart trusts; so I am helped, and my heart exults, and with my song I give thanks to him. (Psalm 28:6–7)

Weeping may linger for the night, but joy comes with the morning. Psalm 30:5b

Be gracious to me, O Lord, for I am in distress; my eye wastes away from grief, my soul and body also. For my life is spent with sorrow, and my years with sighing; my strength fails because of my misery, and my bones waste away. (Psalm 31:9–10)

I will bless the Lord at all times; his praise shall continually be in my mouth. My soul makes its boast in the Lord; let the humble hear and be glad. O magnify the Lord with me, and let us exalt his name together.

I sought the Lord, and he answered me, and delivered me from all my fears. (Psalm 34:1–4)

God is our refuge and strength, a very present help in trouble. (Psalm 46:1)

Be still, and know that I am God! I am exalted among the nations, I am exalted in the earth. (Psalm 46:10)

For God alone my soul waits in silence, for my hope is from him. (Psalm 62:5)

Let your work be manifest to your servants, and your glorious power to their children. Let the favor of the Lord our God be upon us, and prosper for us the work of our hands—O prosper the work of our hands! (Psalm 90:16–17)

You who live in the shelter of the Most High, who abide in the shadow of the Almighty, will say to the LORD, "My refuge and my fortress; my God, in whom I trust." (Psalm 91:1–2)

Enter his gates with thanksgiving, and his courts with praise. Give thanks to him, bless his name.

For the LORD is good; his steadfast love endures forever, and his faithfulness to all generations. (Psalm 100:4–5)

O give thanks to the LORD, for he is good; his steadfast love endures forever! (Psalm 118:1)

With the LORD on my side I do not fear. What can mortals do to me? The LORD is on my side to help me. (Psalm 118:6–7a)

I lift up my eyes to the hills—from where will my help come? My help comes from the LORD, who made heaven and earth.

He will not let your foot be moved; he who keeps you will not slumber. He who keeps Israel will neither slumber nor sleep.

The LORD is your keeper; the LORD is your shade at your right hand. The sun shall not strike you by day, nor the moon by night.

The LORD will keep you from all evil; he will keep your life. The LORD will keep your going out and your coming in from this time on and forevermore. (Psalm 121:1–8)

Then our mouth was filled with laughter, and our tongue with shouts of joy; then it was said among the nations, "The LORD has done great things for them." The LORD has done great things for us, and we rejoiced. (Psalm 126:2–3)

Unless the LORD builds the house, those who build it labor in vain. Unless the LORD guards the city, the guard keeps watch in vain. (Psalm 127:1)

How very good and pleasant it is when kindred live together in unity! It is like the precious oil on the head, running down upon the beard, on the beard of Aaron, running down over the collar of his robes. It is like the dew of Hermon, which falls on the mountains of Zion. For there the LORD ordained his blessing, life forevermore. (Psalm 133)

O Lord, you have searched me and known me. You know when I sit down and when I rise up; you discern my thoughts from far away. You search out my path and my lying down, and are acquainted with all my ways. Even before a word is on my tongue, O Lord, you know it completely. You hem me in, behind and before, and lay your hand upon me. Such knowledge is too wonderful for me; it is so high that I cannot attain it. (Psalm 139:1–6)

If I ascend to heaven, you are there; if I make my bed in Sheol, you are there. If I take the wings of the morning and settle at the farthest limits of the sea, even there your hand shall lead me, and your right hand shall hold me fast. (Psalm 139:8–10)

The Lord is good to all, and his compassion is over all that he has made. (Psalm 145:9)

For the Lord gives wisdom; from his mouth come knowledge and understanding; (Proverbs 2:6)

Trust in the Lord with all your heart, and do not rely on your own insight. In all your ways acknowledge him, and he will make straight your paths. (Proverbs 3:5–6)

Pleasant words are like a honeycomb, sweetness to the soul and health to the body. (Proverbs 16:24)

For everything there is a season, and a time for every matter under heaven:

a time to be born, and a time to die; a time to plant, and a time to pluck up what is planted; a time to kill, and a time to heal; a time to break down, and a time to build up; a time to weep, and a time to laugh; a time to mourn, and a time to dance. (Ecclesiastes 3:1–4)

Those of steadfast mind you keep in peace—in peace because they trust in you. (Isaiah 26:3)

O Lord, by these things people live, and in all these is the life of my spirit. Oh, restore me to health and make me live! (Isaiah 38:16)

But those who wait for the LORD shall renew their strength, they shall mount up with wings like eagles, they shall run and not be weary, they shall walk and not faint. (Isaiah 40:31)

Do not fear, for I am with you, do not be afraid, for I am your God; I will strengthen you, I will help you, I will uphold you with my victorious right hand. (Isaiah 41:10)

The steadfast love of the LORD never ceases, his mercies never come to an end; they are new every morning; great is your faithfulness. (Lamentations 3:22–23)

Blessed are those who mourn, for they will be comforted. (Matthew 5:4)

Blessed are the peacemakers, for they will be called children of God. (Matthew 5:9)

Come to me, all you that are weary and are carrying heavy burdens, and I will give you rest. Take my yoke upon you, and learn from me; for I am gentle and humble in heart, and you will find rest for your souls. For my yoke is easy, and my burden is light. (Matthew 11:28–30)

He said to them, "Come away to a deserted place all by yourselves and rest a while." For many were coming and going, and they had no leisure even to eat. (Mark 6:31)

But now more than ever the word about Jesus spread abroad; many crowds would gather to hear him and to be cured of their diseases. But he would withdraw to deserted places and pray. (Luke 5:15–16)

He answered, "You shall love the Lord your God with all your heart, and with all your soul, and with all your strength, and with all your mind; and your neighbor as yourself." (Luke 10:27)

For God so loved the world that he gave his only Son, so that everyone who believes in him may not perish but may have eternal life. (John 3:16)

I give you a new commandment, that you love one another. Just as I have loved you, you also should love one another. By this everyone will know that you are my disciples, if you have love for one another. (John 13:34–35)

We know that all things work together for good for those who love God, who are called according to his purpose. (Romans 8:28)

I appeal to you therefore, brothers and sisters, by the mercies of God, to present your bodies as a living sacrifice, holy and acceptable to God, which is your spiritual worship. Do not be conformed to this world, but be transformed by the renewing of your minds, so that you may discern what is the will of God—what is good and acceptable and perfect. (Romans 12:1–2)

For as in one body we have many members, and not all the members have the same function, so we, who are many, are one body in Christ, and individually we are members one of another. (Romans 12:4–5)

Do not lag in zeal, be ardent in spirit, serve the Lord. Rejoice in hope, be patient in suffering, persevere in prayer. Contribute to the needs of the saints; extend hospitality to strangers. (Romans 12:11–13)

If it is possible, so far as it depends on you, live peaceably with all. (Romans 12:18)

But he said to me, "My grace is sufficient for you, for power is made perfect in weakness."

So, I will boast all the more gladly of my weaknesses, so that the power of Christ may dwell in me. (2 Corinthians 12:9)

By contrast, the fruit of the Spirit is love, joy, peace, patience, kindness, generosity, faithfulness, gentleness, and self-control. There is no law against such things. And those who belong to Christ Jesus have crucified the flesh with its passions and desires. If we live by the Spirit, let us also be guided by the Spirit. (Galatians 5:22–25)

Bear one another's burdens, and in this way you will fulfill the law of Christ. (Galatians 6:2)

So let us not grow weary in doing what is right, for we will reap at harvest time, if we do not give up. (Galatians 6:9)

Be angry but do not sin; do not let the sun go down on your anger…and be kind to one another, tenderhearted, forgiving one another, as God in Christ has forgiven you. (Ephesians 4:26 and 32)

"Honor your father and mother"—this is the first commandment with a promise: "so that it may be well with you and you may live long on the earth." (Ephesians 6:2–3)

For it is God who is at work in you, enabling you both to will and to work for his good pleasure.
Do all things without murmuring and arguing, so that you may be blameless and innocent, children of God without blemish in the midst of a crooked and perverse generation, in which you shine like stars in the world. (Philippians 2:13–15)

I can do all things through him who strengthens me. (Philippians 4:13)

Bear with one another and, if anyone has a complaint against another, forgive each other; just as the Lord has forgiven you, so you also must forgive. Above all, clothe yourselves with love, which binds everything together in perfect harmony. And let the peace of Christ rule in your hearts, to which indeed you were called in the one body. And be thankful. (Colossians 3:13–15)

For this reason I remind you to rekindle the gift of God that is within you through the laying on of my hands; for God did not give us a spirit of cowardice, but rather a spirit of power and of love and of self-discipline. (2 Timothy 1:6–7)

Guard the good treasure entrusted to you, with the help of the Holy Spirit living in us. (2 Timothy 1:14)

And let us consider how to provoke one another to love and good deeds, not neglecting to meet together, as is the habit of some, but encouraging one another, and all the more as you see the Day approaching. (Hebrews 10:24–25)

Jesus Christ is the same yesterday and today and forever. (Hebrews 13:8)

Humble yourselves before the Lord, and he will exalt you. (James 4:10)

Finally, all of you, have unity of spirit, sympathy, love for one another, a tender heart, and a humble mind. (1 Peter 3:8)

For the eyes of the Lord are on the righteous, and his ears are open to their prayer. (1 Peter 3:12a)

Cast all your anxiety on him, because he cares for you. (1 Peter 5:7)

See what love the Father has given us, that we should be called children of God; and that is what we are. The reason the world does not know us is that it did not know him. (1 John 3:1)

DOCTOR OF MINISTRY PROJECT PAPER BIBLIOGRAPHY

Sources Referenced

Beach, Shelly. *Ambushed by Grace: Help and Hope on the Caregiving Journey by Shelly Beach (2008-11-01)*. Grand Rapids, MI: Discovery House, 2008.

Büssing, Arndt, Daniela Recchia, and Klaus Baumann. "Reliance on God's Help Scale as a Measure of Religious Trust—A Summary of Findings." *Religions* 6, no. 4 (December): 1358-67. http://dx.doi.org/10.3390/rel6041358 (accessed January 13, 2018).

Carson, Verna Benner, and Harold G. Koenig. *Spiritual Caregiving: Healthcare as a Ministry*. Philadelphia, PA: Templeton Press, 2004.

Daly, Jane. *The Caregiving Season: Finding Grace to Honor Your Aging Parents*. Carol Stream, IL: Tyndale House Publishers, 2016.

Family Caregiver Alliance, Caregiving, https://www.caregiver.org/caregiving (Accessed January 15, 2018).

LaGuardia, Joseph V., and Daphne Reiley. *A Tapestry of Love: The Spirituality of Caregiving*. Middletown, DE: CreateSpace Independent Publishing Platform, 2013.

Lu, Lu, Lie Wang, Xiaoshi Yang, and Qiaolian Feng. "Zarit Caregiver Burden Interview: Development, reliability and validity of the Chinese version." *Psychiatry and Clinical Neurosciences* 63, no. 6 (undefined): 730-34. http://dx.doi.org/10.1111/j.1440-1819.2009.02019.x (accessed January 13, 2018).

McLeod, Beth Witrogen. *Caregiving: The Spiritual Journey of Love, Loss, and Renewal*. New York, NY: Wiley, 2000.

Miller, Valeri H. *Who Cares? God's Path for the Caregiver*. N.p.: Valeri Miller, 2013.

Nouwen, Henri J.M. *A Spirituality of Caregiving*. Nashville: Upper Room, 2011.

National Academies of Sciences, Engineering and Medicine, Families Caring for an Aging America, Report in Brief, September 2016.

National Alliance for Caregiving (NAC) and AARP Public Policy Institute, Executive Summary: Caregiving in the U.S., 2015.

National Alliance for Caregiving (NAC) and AARP Public Policy Institute, Research Report: Caregiving in the U.S., 2015.

National Alliance for Caregiving (NAC), From Insight to Advocacy: Addressing Family Caregiving as a National Public Health Issue, 2018.

Portnoy, Dennis. "Burnout and Compassion Fatigue: Watch for the Signs." *Health Progress* (August 2011).

Sadak, Tatiana, Anna Korpak, Jacob D. Wright, Mee Kyung Lee, Margaret Noel, Kathleen Buckwalter, and Soo Borson. "Psychometric Evaluation of Kingston Caregiver Stress Scale." *Clinical Gerontologist* 40, no. 4 (April): 268-80. http://dx.doi.org/10.1080/07317115.2017.1313349 (accessed January 13, 2018).

Sevens Home Care, Activities of Daily Living, https://www.sevenshomecare.com/services/7-activities-of-daily-living/ (Accessed January 15, 2018).

Shelly, Judith Allen. *Spiritual Care: A Guide for Caregivers.* Downers Grove, IL: IVP Books, 2000.

Tourville, Abbé de. *Letters of Direction: Thoughts on the Spiritual Life from the Letters of Abbé de Tourville.* New York: Bloomsbury Academic, 2005.

Underwood, Lynn. *Spiritual Connection in Daily Life: Sixteen Little Questions That Can Make a Big Difference.* West Conshohocken, PA: Templeton Press, 2013.

Willis, Bob. *The Ultimate Caregiver.* Mustang, OK: Tate Publishing, 2008.

Wood, Benjamin T.; Worthington, Everett L.; Exline, Julie Julia; Yali, Ann Marie; Aten, Jamie D.; and McMinn, Mark R., "Development, Refinement, and Psychometric Properties of the Attitudes Toward God Scale (ATGS-9)" (2010). Faculty Publications Grad School of Clinical Psychology Paper 167, http://digitalcommons.georgefox.edu/gscp_fac/167 (accessed January 13, 2018).

Sources Consulted

Abbit, Linda. *The Conscious Caregiver: A Mindful Approach to Caring for Your Loved One Without Losing Yourself.* Avon, MA: Adams Media, 2017.

Briggs, Rick. *Caregiving Daughters: Accepting the Role of Caregiver for Elderly Parents.* New York: Routledge, 1998.

Carter, Rosalynn, and Susan K. Golant. *Helping Yourself Help Others: A Book for Caregivers.* Revised ed. New York: Public Affairs, 2013.

Figley, Charles R., ed. *Burnout in Families: The Systemic Costs of Caring (Innovations in Psychology Series).* Boca Raton, FL: CRC Press, 1997.

Hall, Jan. *Who Cares for the Caregiver?* Middletown, DE: CreateSpace Independent Publishing Platform, 2010.

Harbaugh, Gary L. *Caring for the Caregiver: Growth Models for Professional Leaders and Congregations.* New York, NY: Alban Inst, 1992.

Haugk, Kenneth C. *Christian Caregiving, a Way of Life.* Minneapolis: Augsburg Fortress Pub, 1985.

Hodgson, Harriet. *The Family Caregiver's Guide (The Family Caregivers Series).* United States: Write Life Publishing, 2015.

Jacobs, Barry J. *The Emotional Survival Guide for Caregivers: Looking After Yourself and Your Family While Helping an Aging Parent.* New York: The Guilford Press, 2006.

Levine, Carol, ed. *Always On Call: When Illness Turns Families Into Caregivers*. Updated ed. Nashville: Vanderbilt University Press, 2004.

Lovern, Sandy. *Finding Your Way: A Spiritual GPS for Caregivers*. Birmingham, AL: New Hope Publishers, 2010.

McNeill, Donald P., Douglas A. Morrison, and Henri J. M. Nouwen. *Compassion: A Reflection On the Christian Life*. New York: Image, 2006.

Murphey, Cecil. *My Parents, My Children: Spiritual Help for Caregivers*. Louisville, KY: Westminster John Knox Press, 2000.

Noonan, Nell E. *Struggles of Caregiving: 28 Days of Prayer*. Nashville, TN: Upper Room Books, 2012.

Olson, Marlys Jean. *A Caregiver's Calling: Ministry Experiences of Those Called to Serve the Vulnerable*. Bloomington, IN: West Bow Press, 2013.

Perry, Joan M. S. *Taking Care; Giving Care: Essentials for New Caregivers*. Middletown, DE: CreateSpace Independent Publishing Platform, 2012.

Pratt, Benjamin. *Guide for Caregivers*. Canton, MI: Front Edge Publishing, 2011.

Richards, Marty. *Caregiving: Church and Family Together (Older Adult Issues Series)*. Louisville, KY: Geneva Press, 1999.

Samples, Pat, Diane Larsen, and Marvin Larsen. *Self-Care for Caregivers: A Twelve Step Approach*. Center City, MN: Hazelden Publishing, 2000.

Tirabassi, Maren C., Maria I. Tirabassi, and Leanne McCall Tigert. *Caring for Ourselves While Caring for Our Elders*. Cleveland, OH: Pilgrim Press, 2007.

Tolson, Chester L., and Harold G. Koenig. *The Healing Power of Prayer: The Surprising Connection between Prayer and Your Health*. Grand Rapids, MI: Baker Books, 2004.

West, Susanne. *Soul Care for Caregivers: How to Help Yourself While Helping Others*. Sonoma, CA: Human Sun Media, 2013.

Zurinsky, Laurie. *God's Heart—Your Hands: This One's for You, Caregiver*. United States: Xulon Press, 2004.

ABOUT THE AUTHOR

Rev. Dr. Beryl Dennis is an ordained minister through the American Baptist Churches, USA. She is a cancer survivor and family caregiver. Dr. Dennis is committed to the Gospel ministry and to the spiritual care of family caregivers. Her caregiving journey began as a caregiver to her parents. Always turning to God for help, especially in unfamiliar experiences, Dr. Dennis was inspired to seek an understanding of the spiritual needs of other family caregivers.